ALTERNATE CURRENT

A collection of poems

GAUTAMADITYA SINGH

BLUEROSE PUBLISHERS
India | U.K.

Copyright © Gautamaditya Singh 2024

All rights reserved by author. No part of this publication may be reproduced, stored in a retrieval system or transmitted in any form or by any means, electronic, mechanical, photocopying, recording or otherwise, without the prior permission of the author. Although every precaution has been taken to verify the accuracy of the information contained herein, the publisher assume no responsibility for any errors or omissions. No liability is assumed for damages that may result from the use of information contained within.

BlueRose Publishers takes no responsibility for any damages, losses, or liabilities that may arise from the use or misuse of the information, products, or services provided in this publication.

For permissions requests or inquiries regarding this publication, please contact:

BLUEROSE PUBLISHERS
www.BlueRoseONE.com
info@bluerosepublishers.com
+91 8882 898 898
+4407342408967

ISBN: 978-93-6452-147-5

Cover design: Tahira
Typesetting: Tanya Raj Upadhyay

First Edition: August 2024

Alternate Current | **iii**

Acknowledgements

We would like to begin by expressing our deepest gratitude to Mr. Daniel Green, Gautam's teacher and mentor for his precious time and valuable suggestions. We profusely thank Ms. Lynne Henwood and Ms. Suniti Sharma for proofreading and reviewing these poems at such short notice and giving their valuable inputs. A special thanks to Ms. Shreya Iyengar for helping out with wonderful ideas and thoughts about the final presentation of this book. We would like to express our heartfelt gratitude to Blue Rose Publishing for designing the book cover and accompanying us in the publishing journey.

About the Poet

Gautamaditya Singh was a vibrant, affectionate, curious, intellectual, and spiritual 17-year-old boy who lived in Jaipur, Rajasthan. He passed away recently leaving behind a profound legacy of literary depth. This collection of poignant and evocative verses delve deep into the human experience, binding us all regardless of age, gender, nationality, religion or disposition. This book of poems has been published by his mother and aunt in his memory and as a tribute to him.

He was a well-traveled existentialist, adventurer, and budding musician, who also experimented with songwriting. He displayed an interest in nature photography (seen on pages 6-8) in the book and had a thrilling experience paragliding. Gautamaditya enjoyed long walks with his dog, hiking in the woods, trips to lakes, and journeying to the foot of the Himalayas which led him to have a transformative experience where he connected with nature in a way that made him lose himself entirely in the process. He was interested in understanding what motivates human behavior, and how our psychology can help us transform ourselves, and in turn, maybe help transform others.

Table of Contents

Acknowledgements v
About the Poet vii

Beauty in Opposite Extremes 1
Everything Looks Smaller from an Airplane Window 2
Hill Station... 3
The Power of Fire 4
Walking on a Tightrope 9
I Want to Be Me.. 11
Stepping into the Light 12

Beauty in Opposite Extremes

It goes without saying that the most unexpected things
are the most efficient sources of happiness.
While they can also give you the worst,
they can easily do the opposite.
As often life gets boring, and boredom is more
of a mindset than a feeling and that's when these
unexpected things start to bring light
and they signify the beauty of this chaos.
They are the perfect, just–
without every aspect of the word
still being more accurate than its traditional base.
It always makes you more susceptible to change
which again is a constant in each of our lives.
Nobody's inner person ever changes
but the viewpoints can always be surprising
because many people with good intentions do bad things and
many people with bad intentions do good.
It's safe to say that you cannot be sure about anything
so why not find beauty in the
opposite extremes?

Everything Looks Smaller from an Airplane Window

As I boarded the plane
I saw my city from the clouds
I went insane.
It felt very nice to finally crawl out of the drain
and not be the king of the well
but the peasant of the skies.
All this time
all the lies I told myself
and all the unsuccessful tries
made me see the true size
but don't get overwhelmed by its might
because it's easy to think about the mysteries of life
and hard to find answers to them, so just take a back seat
and look at the world from an airplane window.
Because even if you didn't go through
the flight guidelines,
it's better to ask than to sit there
wondering what comes next
even if there's no one.
There's one common thing.
We all bear the ability
to stare down the airplane window.

Hill Station

The randomness of the universe makes these two feelings
go up and down like a
Hill Station – the roller coaster ride,
like lives we often lead
is very unpredictable
and even if not from a superficial aspect
deep down we all know that change is drastic.
You could be a machine, a toy, a monster, or a piece of plastic.
It all changes, someday when times are different.
Feels like nature is being sarcastic
and even when everything changes
there's still a constant thing.
It's the change itself that turns a pagan into a catholic.
You can fight to deny it all you want, it will just taunt you
in its inevitably amusing ways.
That's why I adjust to the pain and rapture
because it never weighs
more than the infinite greys
produced by an unstable hypocrite called change.

The Power of Fire

Sometimes, you feel a certain way
and you surely don't want to
but you just can't control it.
You sway side to side, climb higher and higher,
just to realize that the rope is oiled
and the quicksand has clenched you harder.
The more vigorously you try to escape
the more vigorous becomes the quicksand.
Then sometimes you feel like
you're soaring high in the sky on a parachute
and you don't want to stop, don't want to get down
but the more effort you put in just to stay up
the lower you get, the slower you want to descend
the faster it gets and you just let go
of the pleasure you were experiencing
just a minute ago. These elements
the earth and the wind are reminders
of the vibrations you feel and cannot control,
the duration of either pain or misery
that accompanies them.
It really just becomes a battle
if you don't know how to leave the baggage

and move forward in the first place
because getting stuck in quicksand
while having extra weight would just make it harder
just like jumping off a cliff on a paraglider
with extra weight would be more dangerous.
It just makes sense that the weight
becomes the bigger problem and not the element,
that's when fire comes to hand,
it can either burn some of the weight
or create more which in return is doused by water
It can pause things for a while
when you just don't know what to do
or where to go and that is when
air gives you a direction.
That can sometimes be misinterpreted,
this proves that it's best
to stick to the earth while doing it.

Walking on a Tightrope

I stood on an edge thinking about the next step.
The sky was so cloudy, it appeared clear.
The wind was so harsh, it felt like it challenged me
to step on the line so, for what it's worth,
it will be my adventure
when the adventurer won't be seen.
This was the primal feeling–
like I had it inside me for centuries.
I wanted to continue thinking
so I could procrastinate my duty.
The duty is to accept all and toss the coin,
heads or tails wouldn't matter.
That's life, they say, just accepting your stakes
and going for the toss.
I could fall or I could walk,
be steady, patient and agile
because honestly, both choices look difficult
but then not taking my chance
not risking all of it for a mere thrill
and again not living a life full of regret.
I had enough.
I took to the line.

My first step felt like walking on the clouds.
The second created a little imbalance.
But by the third one, I knew that it was just a gamble.
You win, you move forward, you lose, you learn.
It felt different, like the best I've had
and more to come ahead because
I'd prefer walking on a tightrope
happily, than doing it forcefully
or refusing the toss.

I Want to Be Me

Running around in circles
I yearn to break free.
What is my next destination–
The mountains or the sea?
I tried to be someone else
but now I want to be me
walking down the rocky shore
compelled and smiling in glee.
Is this a better future I see?
But deep down I know
that the only place where I belong,
where I should be,
is the present–
not the foresight rock
or the hindsight tree.

Stepping into the Light

I'll trade the crowded avenues for open skies
find solace in nature's gentle lullabies
the weight of the past, I'll release and let go
leaving footprints behind, letting my spirit grow.
No more sleepless nights, no more endless fights.
leaving behind the darkness, stepping into the light
as the sun sets on the familiar streets.
Whispered goodbyes and bittersweet retreats
I'll follow the winding roads to the unknown
embrace the uncertainty and make a new home.

Note - Now released into a song under the Title:"Stepping into the Light" (Lyrics: Gautamaditya, Artist: Rishi Vinod and Arranged by Sicra Productions). Available on Spotify, YouTube, iTunes, iHeartRadio, Tik Tok, Amazon Music, Boomplay and several other Apps worldwide.

www.ingramcontent.com/pod-product-compliance
Lightning Source LLC
LaVergne TN
LVHW050853210225
804187LV00016B/331